RHYME
to PASS *the*
TIME

K.B. CHANDRA RAJ

Order this book online at www.trafford.com
or email orders@trafford.com

Most Trafford titles are also available at major online book retailers.

© Copyright 2020 K.B. Chandra Raj.
All rights reserved. No part of this publication may be reproduced, stored in a retrieval system, or transmitted, in any form or by any means, electronic, mechanical, photocopying, recording, or otherwise, without the written prior permission of the author.

Print information available on the last page.

ISBN: 978-1-6987-0290-2 (sc)
ISBN: 978-1-6987-0291-9 (hc)
ISBN: 978-1-6987-0292-6 (e)

Library of Congress Control Number: 2020916202

Because of the dynamic nature of the Internet, any web addresses or links contained in this book may have changed since publication and may no longer be valid. The views expressed in this work are solely those of the author and do not necessarily reflect the views of the publisher, and the publisher hereby disclaims any responsibility for them.

Any people depicted in stock imagery provided by Getty Images are models, and such images are being used for illustrative purposes only.
Certain stock imagery © Getty Images.

Trafford rev. 08/26/2020

www.trafford.com
North America & international
toll-free: 844-688-6899 (USA & Canada)
fax: 812 355 4082

My Dear Reader

Great works have been produced by writers of amaranthine reputation while in confinement.

Machiavelli, "The Prince," Oscar Wilde, "De Profundis," Anne Frank, "The Diary," Cervantes, "Don Quixote."

And this above all. The Bard, "also known as" William Shakespeare, wrote the poem "Venus and Adonis" during the bubonic plague, known as Black Death, when the theaters were shuttered in 1593.

This, dear reader, is my attempt at composing poetry – I prefer to call them "Rhymes"-- during the Covid-19 confinement.

Some feel like humming. Keep humming, friends, if it makes you feel good.

Some pick up the guitar and start strumming because it makes them feel good. Keep strumming, my friends, you are doing good.

Some between chores would pick up the phone and dial a dear friend. The cheerful voice at the other end rejuvenates him or her to no end.

The lark will sing morning and evening, all day the crow will caw, the mosquito will bite, and I, dear reader, though not very bright, must write.

The pages that follow will prove me right.

Please do not say, "This sucks! Could you not do better? We're your readers, remember. So please give us the best you can conjure. We know you have your limits for sure. Provoke our thoughts for goodness' sake. Challenge us for God's sake."

"We don't expect from you Dante's "Divine Comedy," Homer's "Odyssey," charming tales - Brothers Grimm or Hans Christian Anderson. We'll settle for witty Ogden or waggish Belloc."

Something like this you mean:

Roses are red violets are blue.
If you want to visit me, come to the zoo.
These injunctions remember, would you.
Feeding me is taboo.
If you must visit the loo, one finger for pee and two for poo poo.
Reader Dear – East or West, wherever you may be -- I promise I'll do my very best. Even though as I gaze into the mirror when I shave in the mornings my frustration grows ever greater, I know for sure that here's a legend in our time whom nobody else knows.

This book is dedicated to our grandchildren - Neela and Deeran.

Two terrific children, a girl and a boy.
O'er the years there's been
Resilience and Persistence,
Mano Dura, Laughter and Joy.
And now to make our lives blissfully complete
with love and affection, adoration replete,
two healthy, sportive grandchildren
whose love we treasure way beyond measure.
Yeah! a girl and a boy.
"Bendito!" Who could've asked for more?

I have no land to give
Stocks, shares or real estate.
Such is my fate.
So, kiddos, take a chance
With this for your inheritance.

Contents

1. Next Time Do Come 1
2. Author's Supplication 3
3. I'm Lost 5
4. The Originals 7
5. Mama's Request 9
6. To Church You Go 11
7. Exodus 13
8. Spare Me the Pain 15
9. When You Cannot Sleep 17
10. Get One's Just Deserts 19
11. Kindness 21
12. Yakety Yak – Blah, Blah. 23
13. Tired and Weary 25
14. Friendship 27
15. Mighty Lucky 29
16. The Not-So-Young Man from Kotahena 31
17. Straight and Tall 33
18. The Ailing Patient 35
19. Let's Remember 37
20. My friend Maven 39
21. I Became a Catholic 41
22. Sanders and No Other 43
23. Ere I Go Astray 45
24. In Search of a Dentist. 47

25	Best Insurance, God's Assurance	49
26	What Cannot Be Cured	51
27	A Damsel in Distress	53
28	Meeting, Meetings	55
29	The Karmic Cycle	57
30	Making Poetry	59
31	Hurt Your Boss at Your Risk	61
32	Your Secrets	63
33	Words Make A Good Story	65
34	Lucky Me	67
35	A Freebie for You	69
36	Once Done	71
37	Loaded Tongue	73
38	The Virus Hocus Pocus	75
39	Corona Blessings	77
40	Tomorrow Will Be Different	79
41	Where's God, O Where?	81
42	A Life in Brief	83
43	My Wish	85
44	Adversity	87
45	There May Come A Time	89
46	This in the Netherworld	91
47	Changing Jobs	93
48	The Boss	95
49	The Kink in The Doggy's Tail	97
50	Watch out children!	99
51	Under the Palmyrah Tree	101
52	Grampa	103
53	Hobson's Choice	105
54	Have you ever seen?	107
55	The Pain of Others	109
56	A Family Tale for the Ages	111

1

Next Time Do Come

Day time, night time,
Who does not like a rhyme?
Thought I was bright,
Started a web site.
For want of support
Lingered long on life support.

[My web site: backhand.flick@blogspot.com
 Created March 2006
 Cremated Nov 2013
I tried very hard, but only a few did come.]

2

Author's Supplication

Dear Lord!
Give me a sense of humor.
(I promise not to leave home without it.)
Bless me with the humility to see a joke
Even if it should increase my yoke.
And this above all:
Give me the power to see me
As others see me.

3

I'm Lost

I've hunted near, I've hunted far,
I've even looked under the sofa, no bloody luck so far.
I cannot find my keys so I cannot look inside my car.
I asked my wife but she can't hear.
("What?")
She's been like that for over a year.
Now I've lost my glasses, I'm in urgent need.
I must have them now (now) so I can read
before I go to sleep.
I've hunted near, I've hunted far.
No bloody luck so far.

4

The Originals

This was a time when Adam was a handsome youth.
This was a time when he walked with God and they say (smile) he spoke the truth.
This was a time when Eve was comely and curvaceous – sensuous and desirous, too. True?
This was the time there was a tree, and there was a fruit.
God, the eternal spoiler, said to Adam and to Eve, "You may dance and you may play the whole day and night too, but here's one thing you must never do.
Taste the fruit? No can do."
Now as I have said, Eve was pretty and Adam an itty- bitty naughty.
Said pretty Eve to naughty Adam, "I am hungry and I know, yum–yum, so are you. I'd rather be a nun if we cannot have fun. Pluck it; let's eat it."
So pretty Eve and naughty Adam ate the forbidden fruit in the middle of the garden.

Good God, the spoiler, was down in a trice and demanded his price, and the two in birthday suit bending low wailed, "We beg your pardon – please, please."
In a thunderous tone the spoiler said, "If it's food you want, you shall henceforth fend for yourself," and he booted them both out with a dreadful roar and barred the door.
You know the rest.
Adam began applying for jobs from ship to shore (BRO, DON'T I KNOW) and Eve was landed with all the chores.

5

Mama's Request

I was not on my best, I must confess.
So my mama today while at play ordered me to rest posthaste.
She sternly said, "Giddy up, girl; rest's what you urgently need."
Sorry to say, I paid no heed.
You know why, folks?
Cause when "REST" is an order
I'm bullied to obey, it won't seem like rest anymore.
Rest then becomes a nettlesome chore.
Sorry, Mama, your order I'm going to ignore.
I've never acted thus before.
Papa! I love you even more.

6

To Church You Go

Some go to church to supplement
their daily walk.
Some go to church just to laugh and talk.
Just for a lark.
Some look forward to the happy conversation
after a painful peroration.
Some go to church for observation.
Some, I would guess, for speculation.
Some to get out of their nest in their Sunday best.
I'm hoping some do go for God's adoration.
The Lord ordered we rest on Sabbath day.
So I lie in bed all day Sunday.

7

Exodus

That itty bitty, pretty, teeny tiny island in the Indian Ocean.
They came from a distant island
Where once prevailed peace and harmony.

They came for reasons diverse,
For better and for worse.
The old from roots torn,
Despondent and forlorn,
Wishing they'd rather be gone.
The young to ply their trade and
worship at the foot of Mt. Mammon.
The middle misfits with closed eyes
To roll the dice and hope galore.
Still others propelled by a force they
Understand no more.

They came from a distant island
Where once prevailed peace and harmony.

They arrived quite unlike in the Ark,
Not two by two and not for a lark.
Some single, oh so solitary,
Some soon aft swift matrimony--
Daddies, mommies, kiddies, kit caboodle,
The whole family tree you see.

They came from a distant island
Where once prevailed peace and harmony.

Daddies, mommies, kiddies, kit caboodle,
The whole family tree you see.

They came from a distant island
Where once prevailed peace and harmony.

They set foot on a foreign land,
Gave each other a loving hand.
In the new country
They longed for Old World
"machan" brand of company.
Clinging to one another
Like mountain climbers,
They strived together,
Sheltered each other
Come winter or warm weather.

They came from a distant island
Where once prevailed peace and harmony.

The dark clouds have rolled by,
Storm followed by clear sky.
The toils and travails a receding memory.
So, they now carp and cant and holler
Because they no longer need the other.
Like butterflies from cocoons they flee.
Fie. Fie. Tweedledum cares not for Tweedledee.

They came from a distant island
Where once prevailed peace and harmony.

This, dear friends, is nothing new,
It all happened before,
It happened to them "Waspies,"
Happened to them from Sicily,
Will happen long after you and me.

They all came from a distant island
Where once prevailed peace and harmony.
They came leaving behind to stew.
Alas! Alas! Abel, Cain and Country, too.

8

Spare Me the Pain

My childhood home I hope to see again.
I used to go from Colombo to Jaffna by "Gandhi Class" train.
And sadden will I with the view?
I keep asking again, again, and over again.
Memory is bound to crush my brain,
and tear asunder my heart, too.
Did not Thomas Wolfe caution, "You cannot go home again"
'cause it will never be the same.
I fear loving memories will zap my brain
and tears will for sure tear my heart in twain.
So, LORD please (please) spare me the pain.

9

When You Cannot Sleep

When you are old and gray
and cannot sleep,
Get into your big armchair
and bury yourself deep.
Take any one of Chandra's books
and slowly read.
Tylenol, Nyquil and Zzzquill
You'll not need.
"Abracadabra" you'll be in deep sleep.
This take notice.
Should nightmares bother you
swiftly call the police.
Check first whether Chandra's around,
He's well known to flee town.

10

Get One's Just Deserts

To the clock a luminous face.
(not about face)
The chair a straight back
(not hunched back)
The table four sturdy legs
(two will not do)
The bell a tongue
(that does not wag)
The cup a lip
(that does not slip)
The cave a mouth
(without Alibaba's thieves)
My head that's seen plenty of wear and tear,
more hair like a bear.

And to you and me, dear friends,
a cheerful, forgiving heart.

11

Kindness

If loving kindness be not shown
To family, friends and
even feuding foes in pain,
To waiters, workers, widows alone,
The old, the feeble and infirm,
Pray what purpose in life,
What gain?
Lord, I'd not want to pass on
with the curse and mark of Cain.

12

Yakety Yak - Blah, Blah.

From the safety and cuddly comfort
of Mother's womb
Wherein there was never a need
to cry for my feed,
(Call me Jolly, Polly or Molly)
I would ride with not a care for Time or Tide.
BLIMEY!
I was pulled out into a lighted room
By men and women with Corona masks,
Ashamed perhaps of their tasks.
The hustle and bustle I now hear
Is far, far too much for my ear.
Why don't they simply slip me back
where I will hear no more yakety yak.
Life was so pleasant inside Mother
I shall never – ever want another.
Yakety yak – blah blah.

13

Tired and Weary

I am so tired and weary,
Has not been easy,
You know better than me.
The journey has been long-drawn.
All my childhood friends going or gone.
The many hard years behind me
With all the loved ones forever gone
Makes me long for the dawn.
How long, God, must I still labor on?
While I'm in supplication knee-deep,
Appears, God, you've gone to sleep.
I hear not a peep.

14

Friendship

Much have I traveled over land
and sea from World War Two
to Corona Nineteen,
And this much have I seen:
A friend in need is a friend indeed.
No matter the color, caste or creed.
The whole world's your eager friend
so long as your riches last.
As soon as handouts cease,
So soon does friendship die.
No need he has for thee.
Does not the calf desert the cow
Whose udder has gone dry?
And do not birds flee a withered tree?
That's how life's been, my friend,
and will always be.

Pray pause in this verse.
It never happens in obverse.
The cow will forever care for her calf
In times good, bad or worse.

15

Mighty Lucky

I've been mighty lucky,
Kind of Ducky – Ducky;
I am healthy to travel everywhere.
Made a little money, not a lot to spare,
And spent it like I don't care.
Please, God, pay heed:
A few more good years is all I need.
So please, please, Lord,
Send urgently a few more good years,
Some dollars and a ticket for two.

16

The Not-So-Young Man from Kotahena

There was a not-so-young man from Kotahena
From the tiny island in the Indian Oceana.
Wanted in a curious manner
To end the hassle of Corona.
So he nicked a hole in an electric pole.
But alas,
Failed to electrify his Chiquita banana.

17

Straight and Tall

It matters not whether I am weak or not,
I'm determined to stand straight and tall.
Whoever said life was going to be easy?
(Easy? How about messy!)
Life has always been for me a struggle.
Never without a tussle.
Yet by the grace of God
I've always come out of it straight and tall.
You believe this guy full of guile?
This is a tall tale with a long tail.

18

The Ailing Patient

A patient getting from bad to worse
Was seen peering into his purse.
"What bewails you, Sir," asked the kindly nurse.
Replied the friendly patient, "I must go home now, nurse,
even if it should be for the worse."
"Take it easy, gentle sir,
You must first finish the course."
With teary eyes and trembling voice
the ailing patient said,
"For me you've done the very best,
Performed every prescribed test.
You're better than the best.
Sorry, kind nurse,
I must be on my way, no other way,
For I've come to the very end of my purse."

19

Let's Remember

They marched to our drumbeat,
Jigged to our every tune,
Nursed us at infancy,
Nurtured us through many moons.
They winced at our pain,
They wailed over our woes;
Unrewarded they departed
Like foot soldiers of old.

Some we met by chance, some by choice.
They touched our hearts and graced our lives.
Like the moon and the stars from dusk light up our night
At dawn sans a cheer fade out of sight,
These friends who by candor and comport mellowed us all
Have been called to that sublime abode of no recall.

Families saddened by separation, stoking
flickering memories of happy bygone days.
Sorrowing homes once filled with frolic and laughter
Pray the tide just once more turns in their favor.
Ailing elders in monastic isolation
Measuring out time, here now, what hereafter.
Kids in shelters dressed in our discards
Hold in their hands the cosmic cards.
No Ace, no King, no Queen. Not even a Jack.
Teary eyed and trembling hands they wonder
Yonder in High Heaven, Why, o why
Has he turned his back?
So, midst the merry din of dizzy glasses,
Above the babel of flippant banter,
As the seconds race towards the zero hour,

Betwixt unborn tomorrow and dead yesterday,
Like fountains hopes rise for another new year.

Dancers are holding hands for the band
to strike their favorite number.
Dance till dawn if you wish, kick your cares away.
Pray, pause awhile, on this day in December,
Let's Remember!

20

My friend Maven

My friend from New Haven
His name is Maven,
Longed to settle down in Heaven.
Masks he did not wear
Washing hands, he did not care.
When asked why, did reply
"I want to settle down in Heaven."
And off he went to Heaven
in the wink of one eye, the other eye
long ago had bade bye - bye.
Good God, passing by one bright summer's day,
When all the little angels were at play,
Seeing Maven cry, asked, "Why, Maven, why?"

And this was Maven's sobbing reply.
Naughty girls there are none,
And, Lord, all the pubs are closed
long before eleven. Not my idea of Heaven.
Send me back to Earth but, please Lord, not to New Haven.
Pray why, Maven, why not to New Haven?
You could go to Yale. I thought you
would be wagging your tail.
This, Lord, is my little tale.
Long enough have you known me
to know I'm no telltale.
All those living outside New Haven, Lord, come to Yale,
And those from New Haven go to jail.
That's how my friend Maven, formerly from New Haven, from
Heaven ended up next-door in Hamden, far from Heaven.
Cheers, Maven!

21

I Became a Catholic

Here's why.
Wherever jolly Catholic men and women combine,
In premises confined or unconfined,
There's always loud laughter, happy chatter,
back and forth banter and (smack your lips)
good red wine.
Take my word it's always so.
BENEDICAMUS DOMINO
Make mine a MERLO

22

Sanders and No Other

(Itty bitty a little late, my little brother.)
Let's reverse the social order
(It's about time, my fellow traveler.)
For those who've had it so much harder.
Down with the bumptious boss,
His necktie collar and pocket
too much dollar.
Let the caring caregivers,
neglected first responders,
teachers and nurses rule.
Wouldn't it be cool
for a change to see
cleaning ladies carefree
gossiping around the pool,
and our cocksure bosses packed off
to a correction school.
Sanders, Sanders, my brother, and no other.

23

Ere I Go Astray

I came into this world with
no shares, stocks or real estate.
And depart I will that-away.
No wrappings with swanky bows.
I am who I am from my tiny head
to my fat toes.
They say I tend to speak my mind
and even teensy testy from time to time.
I am not a cardiologist, neurologist or virologist,
Didn't care to be or (shame on me) couldn't be.
I believe you can be you and I can be me.
That's how we were all meant to be.
I try to stay strong when the old one - two
socks me down.

I do cry only (between you and me) when no one's around.

To err is human I've heard people say.
Tell me: Who's perfect anyway?
Please, Lord, show me the way
Ere I go astray.

24

In Search of a Dentist.

I've lived in many towns, up-town, mid-town and down- town, too.
Have searched from man to womankind.
A good dentist is hard to find.
Now I've found one that's caring and kind.
But it's the paying I do mind.
I wish they had background music to relax.
Instead of the yakety-yak-yak I hear behind my back.
I am glad I don't have to return for a while.
Thank you for giving back my Marilyn Monroe smile.

25

Best Insurance, God's Assurance

Time's I've been with hardship beset.
My spirits have been unsteady, slippery and sopping wet.
Friends and family sorrowing for me,
their mood's been stark black.
Determined was I not to rest on my back.
I lived each day by a simple plan.
"Pray, what plan, young man?"
Enjoy life but live clean, kind of
as much as you can.
Lived each day as if my last.
Believe me, life was a blast.
Yet faith in God I did not lack.
With little help from above,
Thanks pal, I turned the clock back.
My friends and family, bless them!
Their sweet mood's back on track.

26

What Cannot Be Cured

For miniature saucers, curios, jugs and vase
and dainty trivialities, sorry chum, there's no more space.
So, the gift is pretty I say
to a friend who had come to stay.
Pray, tell me, how much did you pay?
I promise to display
at least while you are here, anyway.
Will that be long?
Your family stringing along?
Last time was pretty long.
Hope, buddy Jerome, you left the
bugs back at home.
The ones you brought last time
continue to roam from room to room
right here in our home.
To be polite, nice and easy (frankly he's a bit of a pain)
to my buddy I hint,
"Your wife must be missing you."
He tugged at his beard – it was worse than I feared:
"What! She's coming here to join you, too."

27

A Damsel in Distress

To dye or not to dye, that's the question.
Whether 'tis nobler in the mind to suffer
the stares and snickers of passers-by
or to take up mask and gloves,
against the virus, the germ, the worm,
and proceed to the hair salon nearby.
Aye, there's the rub.
To dye and then to sleep. No more?
To sleep? Perchance to dream?
In that dream would I grunt and sweat and dread impending death?
Or bear boldly the whips and scorns of conscience. Shuffle off this
pestilential conscience and proceed pronto to the hair salon.
To dye or not to dye remains the question.
Thus conscience, fickle conscience, finger-wagging conscience,
makes cowards of us all.

28

Meeting, Meetings

His wife's chairman of many committees,
Meetings from dawn to dusk.
While her spouse (poor Gus) must settle for
scrambled eggs, stale toast and rusk.
When asked why the furniture's covered
with so much dust, would reply in raw disgust,
"What is pomp and glory,
President, prince and pauper,
Ashes to Ashes – Dust to Dust,
And die we all must, and when we go
We make more dust.
What big fuss?"
The furniture (of course) continues to be covered with dust,
And poor Gus until he turns to dust
must settle for scrambled eggs, stale toast and rusk.

29

The Karmic Cycle

This karmic cycle in which we come and go
Again, and again come and go,
(i.e. if you believe it to be so)
The wise with grey beards have said, "We know not whence we come or why,"
Appears to have neither a beginning nor a final end.
Will someone do tell me truthfully like a friend, even if you are a foe,
Whence we have come and wither do we go?
Strange is it not, dear friend or foe, that those who gave
us life and limb and loved us true
Have passed that same door of darkness through
And yet not one – not one -- has returned to tell us of the road.
To discover (pray) must we travel the same road too?
As for me I'm willing to wait till the moon turns blue.

30

Making Poetry

I've tried everything from left to right, up all night.
Nothing's coming right.
I say, "Better throw in the towel tonight."
Just then:
"Dear," I hear my wife call,
"It's almost midnight."
I go to bed sans paper, pen or light.
Now the words come and dance before me right within my sight.
The cheek! Sits close to me tight and mocks me
throughout the night.
It's true.
No sooner you close your eyes the words are sure to come teasing you.
Tell me true, what should I do?
This is what I should do but seldom do:
Lord, give me grace again and then again the words I long for will pour from my vein like rain on parched terrain.

31

Hurt Your Boss at Your Risk

Indulge in no angry futile wish
to hurt your boss thinking you can.
This never forget, young man.
Forever the chickpea, thinking it can, hopped up and down and up
and down yet failed to crack the frying pan.
If you continue to hold your foolish ire,
You'll end up like all the others,
From the frying pan into the fire.

32

Your Secrets

Whatever secrets men shelter
are revealed helter skelter
when drunk or talking in their sleep.
So, here's a tip.
Not that I know, I've heard it so.
If you wish your secrets keep,
Take not a swig and sleep with your partner.

33

Words Make A Good Story

Somewhere in a burst of glory,
Sometimes in a mood a little hoary,
Sound in my heart's longing to become a song;
Alas! sob–sob (in my case) not for long.
But words for me, ha–ha, make a good story.

34

Lucky Me

When life's storm clouds surrounded me,
A lonely fisherman in the night far out at sea,
When life like crackles and flashes of lightning
and thunder in a burning sky scared me,
When my heart was filled with fear and uncertainty,
When my shoulders were too weak
for the burdens placed on me,
When all the roads were blocked for me,
When all the doors were bang-shut and bolted on me,
I kept asking, "For Heaven's sake, why me – why me?"
Someone from somewhere (always) sent help for me.
Now I am grinning, ear to ear, yep year to year.
LUCKY ME.

35

A Freebie for You

This I give to you a freebie
I've had a belly full of:
"I should have, I would have, I could have."
I've cast them all out of my vocabulary.
Now I'm free.
You should try it out, believe me,
You too will be free.
This advice comes with a lifetime warranty.

36

Once Done

Once done cannot be undone, wise folks say.
Little Anne Frank from her hideout in Amsterdam did supplicate,
You do not have to repeat the same mistake anyway.
That's the lesson that must come to stay.
Wise girl. By precept and practice she showed us all,
the Right Way.
With patience and fortitude, she stuck it out all the way.

37

Loaded Tongue

The use of tongue has been made a crafty art.
Beware and Behold!
In the heat of passion and provocation
Harsh words have cut short friendly, spirited conversation,
Soured friendship and kept us forever apart.
A shame.
The camaraderie will never be the same.
Tis true the loaded tongue, dear friends, is to be feared more than a loaded gun.

38

The Virus Hocus Pocus

The virus has played havoc on all of us.
Charlie has no longer a job like most of us.
He steals 'tis true, but only food,
And that he takes home for his brood.
Living hand to mouth put little to nothing aside,
He's forced to steal so his family can survive.
Guess we'd do the same so our family
can stay alive
Until at least better times arrive.
So next time you see a fellow filching food,
dear friends, do please look the other side.
Whisper! Say it like a prayer,
"There but for the grace of God go I."

39

Corona Blessings

Corona is a blessing to you and me.
Think I'm crazy?
Follow me.
Life has become relaxed and tension free.
Dress casually, chew your food leisurely, consume your coffee sippy- sippy and work from home where your boss can't see.
Isn't that a luxury?
Forced to spend time indoors daddies are getting to know mommies and mommies daddies, and kiddies their mommies and daddies like never before.
Children are spending more time with aging parents – they always wanted to but could not find the time heretofore.
Choice homemade food is the order of the day.
Improvisation and conservation have come to stay.

Wait! Conservation did you say? Wasn't that what our parents used to teach us all the way?
Cupboards are arranged, drawers are cleaned,
Free time used effectively.
Doing all the things you wanted to do previously.
People are spending more time indoors,
coming closer and together like never before.
Roads are deserted, driving at leisure,
Never can remember when we had such pleasure.
Libraries are closed, books are coming out of dusty cupboards.
So are paint brushes and watercolors.
Happily, we have become so art conscious.
Toiled hard, working from eight to five and built a house to retire in but time just flew by.
Thanks, dear Corona, am now savoring the time in the house I worked long and hard to pay for but rarely had the time to enjoy.

People have become more health conscious.
Mommies can be heard constantly calling,
"Wash your hands, wash your hands, my precious."
Friends from around the globe keep calling.
Friendships renewed so much to our liking.
Zoom meetings are booming, can now chat in home clothes while eating and drinking.
Dressing for church will be a thing of the past.
God will zoom into our drawing rooms at last.
Belittle not sayings of old;
As promised, the mountain has come to Mohammed. Behold!
Corona statistics have reminded us life is short.
So, let's make the most of what we've got.
Bless your heart.

40

Tomorrow Will Be Different

Today is different than it was heretofore.
There's a rush for toilet rolls like I have never seen before.
A mad frenzy to buy and buy, there's not much left in the store.
Let not time hang on your hands – be not indifferent.
Read, write, be productive, hoping and praying
tomorrow will be different.

41

Where's God, O Where?

Chanting and singing, humming and hawing,
Prostrating and meditating,
Brother, no one's heeding.
Open your eyes and look everywhere,
And for God's sake stop kidding.
Show me God if you dare. Nowhere, brother, nowhere.
He must be somewhere?
He is everywhere.
The fireman with an axe who puts his life on the line
to save many lives and no axe to grind.
The nurses and doctors tending to Corona patients who are dying
to save patients from dying.
The paramedic who comes screeching to a place of accident to aid one in distress surrounded by onlookers under stress who don't know what to do. Not a clue.

The guy who goes from door to door delivering your online order risking his life so his family can survive.
The smiling elderly lady you see every day stopping traffic with feeble hands to let little children pass by, she whose name you and I cannot say and does it all for no pay.
The guy who picks you up when you have slipped on the sidewalk, dusts you off, and walks away as it happened to me one day – you'll never recognize him again anyway. The "Good Samaritan" all the way.

42

A Life in Brief

I have marched to a different drummer, all my life I have danced to a different tune, not always by choice.

I have seen war in Malaysia and driven into the jungle with no one to mingle – a place called "Sungaituwa."

In shock and shivers I've spent long hours in dark musty shelters (not above ground) while bombs like grapes in clusters were falling all around.

I've seen Japanese soldiers amble past our house, large, sharp swords dangling by their waists with their right hand free to slice your neck with glee.
They have done it to many, believe me.

I'm amused when I hear parents complaining
their children haven't been to school for four weeks or more. I had not been inside a classroom for four years but I wasn't complaining. Played cricket on the street, believing I'd be Don Bradman someday.
That was, I admit, a big price I had to pay.

Caught in the crossfire of communal riots in Ceylon, I had nowhere to stay except the Y.M.C.A. Confessed, "Sir, I'm not Christian." The manager, Mr. Weerasinghe, said smiling, "That's O.K."

Worked in Liberia when Master Sgt. Samuel K. Doe assassinated President Tolbert and pandemonium galore. Huddled in a friend's home (Thank you, "Uncle Chels," thank you) while soldiers went from door to door.

Grabbed my Chevy away at gun point
only to ditch it on their way.
He was looking for a better, bigger car, I dare say.

Saw my neighbor, the minister of agriculture, handcuffed behind
his back and taken away.
Was seen swinging from a lamp post in the
light of day.
The wife bringing food for him was on her way.

Like a good fighter pilot, I returned to base – to Ceylon – sorry,
now Sri Lanka, Serendib and Ceylon no more.

Communal discord began heating up once more.
Seems to follow me wherever I go like the tropical shadow.
Handed house keys to the caretaker, not anxious to make early
acquaintance with the undertaker, bolted to Sierra Leone. Ah! that
beautiful country along the Atlantic shore.

Now here I am with kith and kin, kit and
caboodle in Connecticut, the land of steady habits for ever more.

Oh No.

These are Corona days. I'm going through it all over again once
more. Oh no, oh no. This time I have nowhere to go.

What have I learnt from all this you ask me, and I say unto you:
Don't complain. It's all pre- ordained.

43

My Wish

I wish I were a poet, a writer of Shakespeare and Steinbeck caliber with a pen of gold.
I wish I had clear access to their thinking, their style in writing, that's been everlasting, mature and bold to behold.
I've looked for inspiration in their writing which to me was haunting, alas brief, and when I tried, my hand was found to be wanting.
I wish I could be a poet, a writer of Shakespeare and Steinbeck caliber with a pen of gold, but sadly I confess I am weary, frail and perhaps a little too old.
Looking longingly, lovingly at my pen no way made of gold, with teary eyes I whisper with a whimper to my doleful and dejected Muse,
"My pen is of no use."

44

Adversity

Ye who have met with adversity's blast,
Whose heads have been bloodied and bowed by its fury,
To whom the twelve months past,
Were as harsh as a tainted and prejudiced jury –
Hold on to your faiths please, join in our chime,
And shout out to thine gods of any kind
For a kindlier time in fair exchange.
Remember the only thing permanent is change.

45

There May Come A Time

There may come a time in our life when all our visions, hopes, dreams of a better life will seem dark and dismal.
There may come a time in our life when we will feel the walls closing in.
There may come a time in our life when we see nothing but hopelessness and despair.
Disenchanted, down and out and singing the blues.
A hand will always reach out to us to lift up our spirits.

46

This in the Netherworld

I witnessed this happen in the Netherworld which I was privileged to visit one day. Had to return to Earth after a brief stay. I have nightmares of what I saw to this very day.
It was a dark and dismal day.
I saw two dead boys silently rise from the grave.
I had observed them quarrelling all night, all day.
With smoke coming out of their noses and fire from their eyes they swore they'd settle their differences today.
Remember Earth laws do not apply in this place.
I hoped I'd rather be in some other place.
Back to back the two faced each other,
Walked ten paces from the other.
In a flash drew their pistols, shot each other.
A deaf cop on the beat heard the noise.
Took aim and shot dead the two dead boys twice.

If you do doubt what I'm telling you to be true,
Just ask the blind man who happened to stand nearby.
He swore to the judge he saw it, too.

47

Changing Jobs

Wisely move your left foot,
The right firmly hold
Just as kids we were told.
Till assured of a new job
Never leave the old.
Believe me!
I am old enough to know.
Have been there many times before.

48

The Boss

A boss pompous, proud and picky,
And slow with the salary
Will for sure see his staff flee
As birds a withered tree.
A boss may holler and scold
And yet his staff he will hold
If he would pay the dollar on the dot
As a matter of duty.

49

The Kink in The Doggy's Tail

No wealth like health in abundance.
And like illness no bitterer foe;
(Don't we now know?)
No love like loving children
And grandchildren even more;
Like ingratitude stabs (ouch) no woe.
Where no great reward is assured,
Where defeat is all but sure
Start not a quarrel.
Be wise, just stay put in a barrel.
Caress and care and cuddle a bum as you will
A bum if he was, a bum he will remain still.
Many have tried only to fail,
Just try to take the kink from a doggy's tail.

50

Watch out children!

"Colossus, Cyclops, Spartacus!
They do not bother us, Grampa,
come and sit with us."
What a mighty creature this virus;
There's no end to what it's doing to us.
Too small to be seen,
too scared to come out clean.
By any name it's dangerous,
Determined to destroy us,
Wipe out the human race.
So let's pray the vaccine race will pick up pace
Before this virus (hocus pocus) kills all of us.
Thank you, my poppets, too soon to think of
"Rest in Peace."
Now where did I leave my earpiece?

51

Under the Palmyrah Tree

Many a time have I sat under the Palmyrah tree in my home country sipping toddy. A little itsy-bitsy tipsy, I agree.
And many times thought seriously what I wanted to be.
Win a Hospital Sweep lottery of a million rupees?
Had no fascination for me.
The gift of wisdom and brains of renowned scholars?
Adam Smith, Erasmus or Copernicus, Amadeus or Pythagoras?
Did not excite me.
A long, happy and healthy life?
That's for old farts, you see. Not me.
A peaceful family life free of pain and strife?
Not on my life, did not even occur to me.
I am a bachelor born to be free.
For God's sake, man, what in Heaven's name do you want to be?
I love adulation, world-wide recognition, loud cheering spectators' admiration, caps in the air without a care screaming and waving, a Pele, a Beckham, a Don Bradman, Viktor Barna or Richard Bergman, the "Brown Bomber" Joe Louis, a Muhammad Ali who "floats like a butterfly and stings like a bee."
That's exactly what I wanted to be.
Now look at me. The good Lord had different plans for me, as you can see.
"Que sera, sera. What Will Be Will Be."

52

Grampa

The old man, a granddad, was seated in his favorite cozy comfy arm chair watching T.V. and dozing in between when he heard two teeny voices call out,
"Grampa, are you there?"
One of them was carrying a book and the two of them together asked, "Grampa, will you read to us?"
Grampa was confused. Looked for his glasses, cleaned them and opened the book.
The three of them then went on a wonderous journey.
To London they traveled and saw Buckingham Palace and the starchy, serious, statue-like guards guarding the palace. And they liked it.
Next, they visited that beautiful country along the Atlantic coast he called Sierra Leone where Grampa had worked for many years. The wide sandy Lumley Beach, large cargo ships passing by.
"Do you know why this country is called Sierra Leone?" Grampa asked and the two replied:
"No, Grampa, tell us, please tell us."
"From the beautiful Lumley Beach, I was describing to you just now, you can see a mountain that looks like a lion; and the Portuguese who first occupied this country called it Sierra (Mountain) and Leone meaning, of course, Lion; and so we have Sierra Leone."
The grandchildren looked at each other and laughed.
"Very funny, Grampa, very funny," they both said.
"How are the people there, Grampa?"
"Very nice, very good to children like you."
The two of them looked at each other and said, "Grampa has been to many countries."

"That's not all, children. I have also worked in a country called Liberia."
"Where's that, Grampa?"

"It is next to Sierra Leone."
"Is it as pretty as the other country, Grampa?"
"You mean Sierra Leone?"
"That's right, Grampa."
"No, not as pretty."
From now on the two grand-children would every Sunday visit Grampa, and he would describe to them the countries and cities he has visited. Paris in France, Geneva in Switzerland, Rome in Italy, Casablanca in Morocco, Murcia in Spain, Eritrea in North Africa, the cerulean Mediterranean and on and on. The two children, glued to their seats, would cling to every word Grampa uttered without interruption.
"One day I will take you both to these places."
"Please, Grampa, please do."
One Sunday when the grandchildren ran to the usual chair. It was empty.
They both ran to the mother and demanded to know where Grampa was.
"He promised to take us to all those beautiful places. Where is Grampa; where is he?" they cried.
"Don't cry children, Grampa is always with you. He's gone ahead and is waiting for you. He loves the two of you. And I know you both love him, too. Now get on with the chores I gave you both to do."

53

Hobson's Choice

At my age problems have I such as these.
Hard to find my glasses,
Hard to find my car keys.
Hard to pee and hard to chew.
The body's begun to droop
and it's getting tough to even poop.

Memories don't seem to last,
Fast becoming a thing of the past.
My hearing's an embarrassment,
My sense of smell and sight has me
in awkward situations.
Now they say I look worse than hell,
As if I was any better before.
Pray tell me what I can do,
Am I to silently suffer these, too?

"Look here," my good friend said,
"Isn't it better than being dead?"
"Considering, dear friend, the sins I have committed, to be dead I surely do dread."

54

Have you ever seen?

A sheet on a river bed,
A single hair on a hammer's head,
Toes on the foot of a mountain,
The eye of a needle wink,
The wing of a building fly,
The trunk of a tree open,
The teeth of a rake bite,
The hands of a clock left or right,
The garden plot deep and dark,
And pray tell me what is the sound
of the birch's bark like?
There's so much left to see
You'll doubtless agree.

55

The Pain of Others

We see all around us doctors and nurses
and first responders die,
Tending to patients as COVID–19 continues to balloon.
Sad to see, the majority of us to the pain of others
are not well attuned.
Did not Shakespeare say years and years ago,
"He jests at scars who never felt a wound."

56

A Family Tale for the Ages

Remember the delightfully eloquent poem by Robert Frost.
"Two roads diverged in a wood...
I shall be telling this with a sigh...
Somewhere ages and ages hence......
I doubted if I should ever comeback...
And that has made all the difference...."
REMEMBER?
My children and children's children
"ages and ages hence,"
I hope you will tell this tale not with a sigh
but with heads held high.
He crossed continents blessed
with the optimism of youth,
the tiger juices flowing,
spurred by giddy ambition,
propelled by a romantic desire to see the world,
intoxicated by the possibilities of a new beginning,
egged on by the hope of an exciting life,
staking all on a single moment, on a fleeting whim,
a fancy, risking everything on one throw at the spinning wheel, not realizing the cosmic dice once rolled cannot be picked up again.
With ten precious pounds sterling in his back pocket, a sporty wife and a two-year old toddler set out to a country that many then referred to as the "white man's grave."
And that, my dear children and children's children, made all the difference.
I hope you will tell this tale not with a sigh but with heads held high.
"Ages and ages hence."

To genial Doug Hawthorne who gave his much treasured time to review my "Rhyme to Pass the Time" many thanks a million times.